PRAISE FOR

ART *is* EVERYWHERE

'Encouraging children to be creative is so important, and Joe is right – ART is everywhere (and in this book)!' LIZ PICHON

'A life-affirming and inspiring book that I wish I'd stumbled across in my formative years.'
RUSSELL TOVEY

'Inspiring! Made me want to dig my old paints out and get creative.'
CHARLIE HIGSON

'A marvellous book brimming with curiosity and imagination.'
DERMOT O'LEARY

'Imagination I fear is under threat in our young people. This book – *Art Is Everywhere* – is a brilliant springboard for young minds who are uncertain about what art is.'
SALLY GARDNER

'What a timely publication this is. We Brits too often forget to celebrate one of our greatest exports – creativity. But with a fun and engaging tone, Joe has an uncanny knack of speaking directly to the middle grade reader and you can feel his excitement as he reminds them how much of the artistic world is at their fingertips. A cheeky little gem.'
BEN BAILEY SMITH

JOE HADDOW

ART

is

EVERYWHERE

illustrated by

ELLIE HAWES

uclanpublishing

Look me up!

Talk to a trusted grown-up before you search for art of any kind online. This includes videos on YouTube, songs on Spotify, paintings on Google or films that have a rating that is for people older than you are.

ART IS EVERYWHERE is a uclanpublishing book

First published in Great Britain in 2023 by
uclanpublishing
University of Central Lancashire
Preston, PR1 2HE, UK

978-1-915235-56-5

1 3 5 7 9 10 8 6 4 2

Edited by Emma Roberts
Text design by Becky Chilcott

A CIP catalogue record for this book is available from the British Library.

Printed and bound in Great Britain by Clays Ltd, Elcograf S.p.A.

To my darling Sam,
for everything

Contents

Hello!

Dear Reader,

Hi, I'm, Joe! I wrote this book you're about to read and, well, I wanted to introduce myself.

From a young age I have loved lots of different forms of **art**, such as drawing, colouring, writing, poetry, music, film, TV. Now, I want to share with you how *joyful* and *inspiring* art can be.

I've been a ***drummer*** since I was nine years old.

When I was eleven I joined my first band, and since then I have always played in one. I've toured the UK on many occasions as a drummer, and even in America too! (More on that later . . .)

I was very lucky to grow up around **books** and lots of other art, because my parents LOVE reading, and my dad is also a *painter*. We had several of his paintings on the walls of our

house, and after I left home, he turned my old bedroom into an *art studio*.

Whenever I go home to visit, I get to see all of his new creations, and what's extra awesome is they're being created in my old room, the place where I used to make **art of my own** with my drums.

Growing up around my dad's art made me **appreciate** it from an early age, and I have since become a small-time collector of modern art.

Similarly with books, **being read to** by my mum and growing up around a little **library** of my own made me a voracious reader and books are now part of my job! As well as being an author,

I do other bookish work like hosting events with other authors, judging national story prizes, and I have a podcast about books too.

I still absolutely luuuuuuuuurve watching films and TV (who doesn't?) and I  have a huge passion for radio, which is, in my opinion, also a form of art.

I studied *radio production* at university, so was constantly recording shows in studios, editing and mixing features and documentaries, and coming up with new creative ideas. I'm now a radio producer, so you could say I have built a **career** from one of my favourite artforms.

All in all, I like to keep my *mind busy* with creative stuff, whether I am creating it myself or enjoying someone else's creations. I really hope that by the time you've finished my book, you might want to do the same. ☺

Happy reading!

Joe x

What is art?

That's a big question – probably too big to start with, actually. Let's try this instead . . .

What do YOU think art is?

I used to think 'art' referred to **drawings** and **paintings** and nothing else. Art was something that hung on the walls of galleries and museums, I thought.

Well, some art *does* hang on the wall of galleries and museums – and drawings and paintings are certainly art – but that little word, those three letters:

ART

cover SO MUCH MORE than *just* drawings and paintings.

Now when I think of *art*, I think of music, books, films, dance, poetry, comedy, fashion, photography, TV and so many other things.

is

where

When I first realised this,
my mind was blown.

I also thought that being an artist meant you had to be able to paint or draw. I thought an artist had a **big canvas**, a **paintbrush**, and was probably wearing a **beret**.

How **wrong** I was about that, too.

So, I can make *music* and be called an 'artist'?

YES, JOE!

Or I could take up *photography* and also be called an 'artist' . . . ?

YES!

This discovery was pretty *life-changing* for me!

Of course, we *do* call people who paint and draw and screen-print and sculpt artists – but there are so many other people who are artists, and I'm going to tell you all about them in this book.

I see artists as being part of a *big worldwide family*, one which I'm very happy and privileged to be a member of – and which, by the end of this book, you may want to join too ...

EVERYONE IS WELCOME!

Tiny klaxon alert! There are a few people who disagree with me on the whole 'everyone is welcome' thing. They're called ART SNOBS, and trust me – we don't need to pay any attention to them.

A **snob** is someone who looks down their nose at certain things in a judgy way.

I knew a snob at school, a boy in my class who thought he had **great taste** in music and always liked to get into arguments about bands and singers. I had listened to an album by a new singer called P!nk – and I **loved** it.

When I told him about it, this was his reaction . . .

'PAH!'

And then he made a face like he'd just smelled something really bad.

'Have you *heard* P!nk's album?' I asked.

'NO, I KNOW IT'S GOING TO BE RUBBISH.'

Snob alert!

The boy in my class *judged* something without even listening to it, because he assumed it wouldn't be good art. But, I had the last laugh there – or rather, P!nk did, as she has gone on to sell more than 100 MILLION records worldwide!

And that's why I want to give you some tips, right at the beginning.

LIKE WHAT YOU LIKE!

No one should feel they have to like something, just because people *say* it's good.

Here's an example – the **Mona Lisa**, by **Leonardo da Vinci**. Do you know this painting? The artist is one of the most famous in the world and the *Mona Lisa* is considered a masterpiece. But, I don't really care for it.

I mean, sure, I appreciate the **skill** that it took to create the painting – and I appreciate that there's a lot of **history** to it – but do I **like** it?

Not really.

Given the option of taking the *Mona Lisa* home or picking something else from the Louvre, the museum it's in, I'd probably go searching.

Many art lovers and critics would think I'm MAD for saying this, but that's OK. Just because **they** love it, and just because millions of others do, it doesn't mean *I* have to.

When I was a teenager I wanted to write a film script – otherwise known as a 'screenplay' – which I would send to  Hollywood and become an overnight sensation. (It hasn't happened yet, but I still have that dream!)

*'**What do people want to watch . . . ?**'* I asked myself, tapping the end of my pencil against my nose and staring at the pages of my notebook.

Here was my ***first mistake***.

Us artists should be making what *we* want, things that *we* think are interesting and exciting and have meaning – not looking to make something just because we think *other people* will like it.*

Art is *subjective*, which means that every single person who creates art will bring their own beliefs and feelings to their work – and so, every single person who experiences that art will do the same.

Not *every* piece of art will be for *everyone*, and that's *great*, because it means there can be space for even more amazing people making incredibly brilliant, *different* things.

*Of course, some artists get paid to make art for other people – which is also fine.

Now, before we **really** get going, I know you'll have some questions, so I have tried to guess a few that I think you'll want to know ...

> **What can I expect from this book then, Joe?**

Well, we're going to look at some creative people I think you'll enjoy finding out about, if you don't know them already.

AND I'm going to give you tips on how you can find your **inner artist** – whether that's putting pen to paper to create your first story, learning a few jokes to tell your friends and family, or getting your dancing shoes on and gearing you up for your best twirl.

I actually know a bit about art – in fact, I already know I want to be an artist – so should I read on?

BRILLIANT! And yes, you should, because one of the great things about being an artist is appreciating fellow artists' work and learning from it.

If I don't know anything about art, is there anything in this book for me?

YES, ABSOLUTELY! We're going on a journey of discovery together . . .

> *Sounds good, what are we waiting for?*

For you to turn the page! ☺

Music

People don't always think of **music** as an art form, but it is! Like most art, it's created from nothing, and built on and changed many times over before it becomes a finished piece.

Think of one of your **favourite** songs . . . Now think of all the different bits that it's made up of.

There's the music, which had to be **composed**, and then all the different **instruments** which had to play the different parts. If you're thinking of a song with **lyrics**, then those words would have been **written** before the singer recorded them. And the singer makes music with their **voice**, too!

AND we mustn't forget the **production** of the song, which is where someone called a producer brings all these bits together to make the song **sound good**.

All of these bits of a song are **art**, and all of them are as important as each other when it comes to the **overall sound**.

Music is also magical! Why? Because it can actually **change** how you feel ...

It can lift your mood, make you feel **joyful** and **happy** and make you want to **dance**. But it can also make you feel **reflective** and make you want to **cry** ...

There's so many different *styles* of music – classical, pop, rap, hip-hop, rock, jazz, soul, country, grime, funk, folk and many, many more – and all of them have the ability to affect our emotions in different ways.

What makes me feel joyful may not make you feel the same way, but that's OK. We're all *different* and we all have different tastes.

For example, I can't listen to a piece of classical music called '*Piano Concerto No.1*' by a composer called *Tchaikovsky* without getting *goosebumps* on my arms! (Tip: if you can find a version to listen to on YouTube or maybe Spotify, listen out for the violins all coming back in together just before the three-minute mark. It's just after the piano has done a bit of soloing, and it's so beautiful, yet powerful. It is, truly, one of the most heart-soaring pieces of music I believe you will *ever* hear.)

And I can't listen to a song called *'Nightshift'* by a band called *Commodores* without smiling and singing along. Commodores were an

American soul group, and this song has such a groove to it, I literally can't not move my feet when I hear it.

So, because music is **magical**, that means the people who make music are **magicians**!

As you know, I play the drums and so, I am obsessed with drummers and drumming and rhythm and beats. In my opinion, drums are the **backbone** of any band – they are the strongest and most important part. The drummer keeps the band playing **in time**, creates the **mood** of the music and is the musician that the rest of the band **follow**. It's a big job!

Did you know **Justin Bieber** plays the drums as well as being a brilliant singer and dancer? I saw him recently in a drum-off with one of my favourite musicians, **Questlove**. (If you haven't seen it, it's on YouTube and it's ace!)

Now, Questlove is *really* talented. Not only is he a fabulous drummer in a band called **The Roots** but he is also a music producer, DJ, film director *and* an author. **Wow!**

His drumming, and love of music, has an influence on the rest of his work, too – like his documentary film, *Summer Of Soul*, about the Harlem Cultural Festival of 1969. The film showcases some incredible live performances from musical artists such as **Stevie Wonder**, **Sly and the Family Stone** and **Nina Simone**.

Another multi-talented musician is **Sara Bareilles**, who I had the pleasure of touring with.

Touring is when bands or singers or comedians travel a country, or countries, performing to people in different towns and cities, in different venues. It's often very fun, but very tiring!

So yes, there I was on tour, travelling up and down the east coast of America. During that tour, I would go onstage to play the . . . wait for it . . . ***suitcase!***

Yep, I drummed on a suitcase, and it was great, because it showed me that you don't have to have an *actual* drum, or drums, to be able to make great rhythmic sounds. My friend David and I only had a small car, so we couldn't fit in a full drum kit, plus, he discovered when you put a microphone into this suitcase, it *boomed* like a bass drum when you hit it at the front and *snapped* like a snare drum at the side. So, we thought it would be fun to try something a little different.

Anyway, back to Sara Bareilles! As well as winning a *Grammy award* for her music (one of the most prestigious awards

a musician can win), Sara's songs have been streamed *millions* of times across the world, she's written the music and lyrics for a musical called *Waitress*, which has been performed on Broadway in New York and the West End in London, AND – on top of all of that – she also wrote a memoir (a book telling the story of her life and career) which became a bestseller! Phew.

Sara loved singing from an early age. She also taught herself *piano* when she was a teenager and began playing small live shows near where she lived. It's quite a big leap from an audience of twenty in those small venues, to performing at the Grammy awards in 2014 with twenty-eight million people watching, isn't it? But, it just shows that every musician starts somewhere, and that *anything is possible*.

Here's another brilliant musician you should know about . . . he's called *Sheku Kanneh-Mason* and he plays the cello.

Sheku won the BBC Young Musician Of The Year award, which led to him signing a *record deal*. He also performed at the wedding of Prince Harry and Meghan Markle, which nearly two BILLION people watched! (How he kept his hands from shaking while he was playing his cello, I'll never know . . .)

Sheku grew up in a musical household. In fact, he has *six siblings* who all play musical instruments, and often perform together.

To hear him play is to be transported into another world. I think the cello is a **beautiful-sounding** instrument anyway, but when the cello is in Sheku's hands, it comes **alive**. The sound he makes with his music gives me those **goosebumps** I mentioned before! See if you can find him playing a piece called **'Nimrod'** by a composer called **Elgar**. It might just give you goosebumps too...

ART IN ACTION

So, *HOW* do I get my music career started then, Joe?

Have you heard an instrument or seen someone playing one and thought – *I like how that sounds*? That could be the place for you to start.

Perhaps you really like the theme tune for a TV show you watch, or a game that you play regularly. Have you ever stopped to listen to it properly or tried to work out which instruments are playing? If not, maybe *give it a try* and see how you get on.

If you're lucky enough to have an instrument already, *keep praaaaactising*! You won't always *want* to practise, but trust me, it's a really good habit to get into. The more you make your art, the better you will be ... *simple as that*!

If you don't have an instrument of your own, your *school* might let you hire or borrow one. It's worth talking to your music teacher about this.

When I first started out as a drummer, I didn't have a full drum kit, but I used some of my parent's old **cushions**. (Using the pans from the kitchen was **not** allowed! I learnt that the hard way . . .) I arranged the cushions so I could practise making my arms and legs do different things at the same time, which is one of the most important things to learn early on if you want to be a drummer.

And of course, you don't have to play an instrument to **enjoy** music. Lots of people simply take a lot of pleasure out of listening to what musicians create. That's one of the greatest things about all art forms – you don't have to able to create it to be able to appreciate it.

 Remember how I said music is **magic**,

because it can change how you feel? Well, have a look at this mini playlist I have put together, which features some of the artists I mention in this chapter. There might be a song you have never heard, which you *really like*.

Look me up!

There might be MORE than one song that you like! And perhaps one of these songs will be the introduction to an artist you want to hear more music from . . .

See if any of these make you feel *happy*, *make you smile*, or maybe even give you those *goosebumps*. And while you're listening, think about what it is about the song that you like (or not).

♥ Is it the *words*?
♥ Is it the *voice*?
♥ Is it the *music*?
♥ Is it a specific *instrument*?

 # JOE'S PLAYLIST

♥ **SUPERSTITION**   **Stevie Wonder**

♥ **EVERYDAY PEOPLE**   **Sly and the Family Stone**

♥ **MY BABY JUST CARES FOR ME**   **Nina Simone**

♥ **LOVE SONG**   **Sara Bareilles**

♥ **CONCERTO IN E MINOR (OP. 85: III. ADAGIO)**   **Composed by Edward Elgar and played by Sheku Kanneh-Mason**

♥ **THE FIRE**   **The Roots**

Writing

Guess what? *Writing* is a form of art! And there's so many awesome types of writing – it could be *poetry*, or *books*, or *scripts* for TV or the theatre, or in *newspapers*.

I try to write *every day*, because, well, I love doing it! But also because writing is actually *good for you* ... like exercise or drinking water.

Clever *scientists* have found that writing can improve your memory and make you *happier*! Sometimes all I write is a little entry in my diary about what I did that day, but that counts.

I also try to *read every day*, to enjoy what *other* people have written. Reading other people's writing can also help us learn things, sometimes ***without noticing***. When we read about other parts of the world, for example, or read about people living a different life to ours, it opens our minds and helps us to imagine what other people might be thinking or feeling. This is called

EMPATHY!

Don't you think it's ***amazing*** that you could be sitting in your bedroom, or in the library, or on the bus, but through the writer's imagination in the book you're reading, you find yourself in a submarine deep under the sea, or in a spaceship speeding through the solar system, or even a mythical land surrounded by wizards!

Whether you prefer **books**, **comics**, **graphic novels**, or even listening to **audiobooks**, they all help us escape from our normal life, and they help us to be CREATIVE!

This is because we are constantly using our **imaginations** when we read a writer's work, so our brains are **buzzing**.

In case you've got a trip to the library coming up, would you like to hear about a few book writers who I love? You might already know of some of them . . .

This is *Liz Pichon*. Hello Liz!

Do you know her books about a boy called Tom Gates?

If so – GREAT! I love 'em. If not – you're in for a treat . . .

Liz actually started out as a *graphic designer* and *artist*, before becoming a writer. One of her first jobs was designing album covers for bands and singers.

She then used her artistic skills to create *characters* by first drawing them, and then developing the stories bubbling away in her head around her drawings. One of these characters was Tom Gates.

If you *have* read a Tom Gates book, you will know that they are full of Tom's hilarious scribbled-down thoughts, and brilliant descriptions of his band. As a musician myself, I love reading about Dog Zombies . . . (That's the name of Tom's band, although dogs that are zombies sound pretty great too!) Liz also draws brilliant doodle-style images throughout her books, which really help tell the story.

If you **haven't** read any of Liz's books before, you could try one called *Shoe Wars*. It's a really wacky story with huge imagination which made me laugh A LOT.

Even though Liz is a grown-up writer, she knows exactly how a kid would talk or think. Her characters, like Bear and Ruby Foot from *Shoe Wars*, or Tom Gates, are very funny but also very *real*. See what you think if you get a chance to read one of Liz's books!

Another of my favourite writers is **Ben Bailey Smith**, who is sometimes known as Doc Brown.

You might recognise him from the **Star Wars** series, **Andor**, (which is for young people of fourteen and older, so check with a grown-up if you want to look for it), or maybe you'll know his voice from TV shows such as *101 Dalmatian Street* and *Thunderbirds Are Go* – because as well as being a writer, Ben is also an actor, a comedian AND a rapper. What a talented man!

I first met Ben when we got to work together on a radio programme (he is *also* a radio presenter) and I just loved how funny and energetic he was. He wrote a book called *Something I Said*, which tells the story of thirteen-year-old Carmichael who stumbles into a career as a stand-up comedian. It's a really funny book!

Ben is *playful* and doesn't take himself or his art tooooo seriously, which I think is a really important thing for any artist to remember. Whether you'd like to write or draw or paint or make music, art doesn't have to be serious. You can have lots of fun and laughs while you create it. (There'll be more on this in our chapter on comedy!)

The final book writer to tell you about is **R. J. Palacio**. (The 'R' and the 'J' in her name stands for Raquel Jaramillo.)

My favourite book of hers is also one of my favourite books of all time ... It's called **Wonder**. Maybe you know it?

It's about a boy called Auggie, an average ten year old, who looks different to other kids and who has never been to a 'real' school before. The book tells his story of joining the new school and how he is treated, both the bad and the good.

The reason I love this book so much is that it's a story about **kindness** and **acceptance** and *friendship*. It's told from different perspectives, which gives the reader a full picture of what everyone is thinking. This helps us understand all the characters' viewpoints,

even if we don't agree with them!
Reading *Wonder* definitely changed
my outlook on life quite a bit.

I also love that Raquel's writing style is
quite simple. She doesn't use ten words
when just one will do and I think that
this makes the story more **_impactful_**
and **_powerful_**. The character of Auggie
and his voice are both very **_believable_**,
and, as a shy, self-conscious person,
his short and sparse dialogue gives the
reader a good sense of how he is feeling.

ART IN ACTION

Right then, Joe, I have a notebook and a pen, so *what* do I do now?

Well, all you have to do now is write! Some writers find it helpful to use something called a *prompt*. This is where they are given the start of a story, and then they use their imagination to think up what might come next.

Do you want to have a go? OK then, here's a prompt from me, just for you:

The last thing Joe had expected to see in a can of baked beans was a snake, but there it was, writhing around in the orangey juice. He dropped the open tin on its side and waited . . .

You could write just a couple of sentences, or pages and pages of a story that starts with this prompt.

Or, perhaps it'll be a short story that you tell someone out loud. Remember that not everything you write has to be perfect first time, and not everything you write needs to stay in your story.

It's OK to write something and delete it later if you decide it doesn't work. ~~I do it all the time!~~

Here's another writing trick you could try the next time you're out and about. Have a look around you and see if you can notice some pieces of writing in places other than books. What about an ***advert at a bus stop*** or on a ***billboard***? Maybe it's something on a ***crisp packet*** or in a ***newspaper***?

Then have a think about how the writing makes you feel. Does it make you ***laugh***? Does it make you want to *ask questions*? Or **buy** something? Does it help you understand how someone else might be feeling?

You see – the art of writing can be spotted everywhere around us!

Contemporary Art

When I look at a painting or photograph that I love, I am **_transported_** . . .

. . . transported away from the room I'm in, from the people, the noises, the time of day . . .

. . . and into the *world* of the painting
or photograph or sculpture, or whatever
it might be that I'm looking at.

All art has this *power*. Like books and music, a great piece of visual art can take you to *another place*, can *lift your spirits* or create an

EMOTIONAL FEELING.

Look around you now . . . is there any art on the walls where you are? Any posters, pictures, photographs or paintings?

Or are there any ornaments, figurines or sculptures? Maybe even a beautifully designed carpet or rug?

Remember how I said that *art is everywhere* . . . ?

Told you so!

Quite often, *visual art* like paintings is put into categories. Perhaps it might be because that art is created in a particular style or at a certain time in history.

'**Contemporary Art**' means work which is being made now, and art that was made in the recent past (the last forty to fifty years).

Do you remember when I said that I don't get all the **fuss** over the *Mona Lisa*?

Leonardo da Vinci started painting it in **1503** (finishing it many years later), and I personally struggle to like a lot of art from that time.

Even though it is one of the most **famous paintings in the world**, and, like I said before, I can **appreciate** the techniques and skills that have been used to produce it, when I look at the *Mona Lisa* I don't feel any **emotion**.

Yes, I KNOW – that's a bit **controversial** . . . but it's the **truth**! (Plus, I bet quite a few people think the same as me but just won't admit it!)

But, as I also said earlier:

IT'S OK TO NOT LIKE EVERYTHING.

Even if a painter, or singer, or actor, or writer, or dancer, or comedian is regarded as being *'one of the best'* – it's all right if YOU don't feel anything when you look at, or hear, or read, or watch their work. Everyone should respect everyone else's tastes and opinions.

WHEN IT COMES TO ART, THERE IS NO RIGHT OR WRONG.

Now then, where was I?

OH YES! *Contemporary art.*

As there has now been many years' worth of contemporary art, it means there's an **awful lot** of artists and artworks to admire. But, because we haven't got a thousand pages in this book, I am going to concentrate on just a few artists that I really love.

Firstly — *Jon Key*.

Jon is an American **artist, writer and designer** from Alabama, in the United States. His work shows the things that he believes make him **who he is** – the fact that he is a Black, queer man, who comes from one of the Southern states of North America, and grew up surrounded by a big family.

Jon started painting when he was *ten years old*, and was always drawn to painting portraits.

He puts that down to being a twin and getting mistaken for his sibling when they were younger.

Now, although his sibling and other members of his family are sometimes the subject of his work, he mainly paints *self-portraits* (pictures of himself).

What I *love* about Jon's work is that as well as concentrating on the four things that make him who he is, it mainly uses

just four colours too, which **represent** one of these four different parts of his *identity*. The colours he uses are green, black, violet and red.

His paintings are bold and striking — they have a *playful element* to them, but are also quite *serious* at the

same time. His characters also have a mysterious *magical realism*.*

*Magical realism blurs fantasy and reality, so that some of the elements of what you're seeing seem perfectly normal, while others are mystical and magical. It's something that can pop up in other forms of art too, like writing.

Jon is also a **teacher** and the co-founder of a group of artists called *Codify Art*, dedicated to creating, producing, supporting and showcasing work by artists of colour. So, not only is Jon a brilliant artist himself, he also **looks out** for other artists and is helping them bring their art to more people. What a guy!

Look me up!

If you want to see what some of Jon's work **looks like**, search for *The Man In The Violet Suit* when you're next on the internet.

Next, I'd like to talk about an artist that you have probably heard of. Most people know this artist's name, even if they aren't into contemporary art. Drum roll please . . .

I am talking about . . . *Banksy*! Have *you* heard of Banksy?

If you have, you'll know that Banksy's identity is a **mystery**, because only a few people in the world actually know who they are!

According to some, Banksy is a male artist and is from Bristol, a city in the west of England.

He began his career by **spray-painting** walls around Bristol and his work went unnoticed for a quite a while, with some people even calling it vandalism instead of art.

But, in the 1990s, when he started using a **stenciling** technique, he began to get more noticed.*

*Stenciling is when you put ink or paint over holes which have been cut into a design or wording. (Stencils can be made in cardboard, paper, or even metal!) Then, the ink or paint form the pattern that the holes have been designed to make, on to paper, or another surface. In Banksy's case, that's brick walls!

Now he's one of the most *famous* artists in the world — and yet, you could bump into Banksy on the street and not have a clue it's him! His work can be seen in many cities across the UK — and in other countries too — and is often *funny*, but with a *serious message*.

I admire Banksy for his street art, but also for the clever stuff he does to make a point to the public.

Here's a cool example of that — at an auction in 2018, where one of Banksy's paintings *Girl With Balloon* was up for sale, the painting suddenly began to shred itself right *after* the painting had been sold for a cool £1.1 million!

The shredder was built into the frame – probably by Banksy – and was believed to have been triggered by the artist himself, right there in the auction house.

Look me up!

The video of it is online and is well worth a watch, just for the shock on the faces of everyone there!

Remarkably, this stunt made the artwork's value soar, meaning the shredded painting half-hanging out of the frame is worth much MUCH more now than it was when it was sold by the first buyer, three days later. (£18.5 million, to be precise!)

Banksy is a **true** artist – someone who doesn't **compromise**, doesn't need **recognition** or **adoration** and who sees everything as an art form, even the way his own artwork is sold.

Banksy has created many iconic images. I love *Sweep It Under The Carpet* too, which is painted on brick and is so clever. But, my favourite is the very simple *If Graffiti Changed Anything – It Would Be Illegal*.

This was painted on a wall near where I used to work – and I was lucky enough to be able to walk past it quite regularly.

The image was of a rat looking up at some words he'd just painted. The words are the same as the name of the painting:

'IF GRAFFITI CHANGED ANYTHING – IT WOULD BE ILLEGAL.'

Banksy's being *cheeky* here, which is very much his style. The wording is suggesting that graffiti *doesn't* change anything (because it is not viewed as an art form by some people).

But, what's clever and funny about this piece is that once the section of wall had Banksy's graffiti on it, it became something of *interest* to the public and worth more money than when it was just plain bricks. SO, graffiti *had* changed it.

When I saw this piece of contemporary art for the first time, it made me *think*, then made me *smile*.

Another artist who was heavily influenced by graffiti, murals and street art is the American artist and creator, *Hebru Brantley*.

Hebru's love of **anime, comic books** and **manga** is very clear in his work – and as a big fan of comic books and

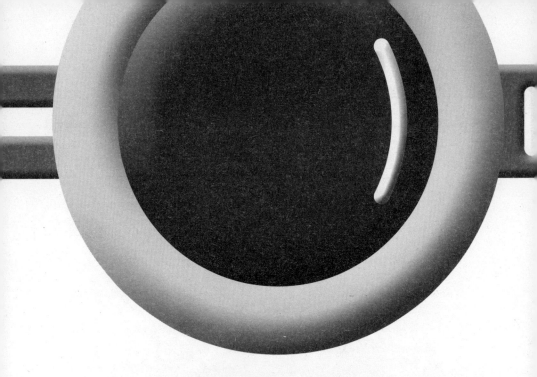

graphic novels myself, is probably why I like what he does so much!

Hebru is the creator of two iconic characters who appear in a lot of his work: *Flyboy* and *Lil Mama*. They are both young, curious and empowered kids who wear flying goggles. I love the vibrancy of these characters and the paintings and drawings they feature in.

Hebru has also made them into **action figures**, which I really love. Wherever and however these characters appear, they are always in **bright colours** and **exciting surroundings**.

The art suggests a sense of adventure (such as Flyboy sitting on a rocket, or in a plane) and there's an **other-worldly** quality to them too.

Another reason why I chose to tell you about Hebru is because, like many contemporary artists before him, his art finds a way into the worlds of **_fashion_** and even **_vehicles_**. It's not just about his paintings or prints hanging on walls, but also about **_collaborations_*** with other creative people and showcasing his art in other ways, like on trainers or cars.

There's also an online store where Hebru sells things like **_T-shirts_**, **_hoodies_** and **_action figures_** – which allows more people to be able to enjoy and experience his work.

**Collaborations are where different people work together on one thing.*

ART IN ACTION

Right Joe, I have a paintbrush and a blank sheet of paper at the ready – what should I do now?

Well, the most important thing to remember is that your first painting, or drawing, or any other piece of visual art that you create ***doesn't*** have to be your masterpiece . . . (Although it might be!) There's no ***right*** or ***wrong*** way to make visual art – it's all about **experimenting** and trying different things.

Do you have a **mirror** in your house? If so, try sitting in front of it and drawing yourself. You can pull a **funny face** if you like! Sketch out the outline of your head and neck, and maybe shoulders too . . . then fill in all your features. Remember, this doesn't have to look exactly like you; as the artist, you have what's called '**artistic licence**' – meaning you can stray away from reality or fact, for artistic purposes. If you don't want to stare at yourself, or you haven't got a mirror available, why not choose an **object** to draw? Pick something fun, but not **toooo** complicated to start with.

Some art supplies, like paint, can be expensive, so you might not be able to start with painting. But not every artist uses paint, or, only paint. There's a very famous artist called *Picasso* who is well-known for his paintings, like *Two Girls Reading*. BUT, some people think Picasso's best work was actually his pencil drawings.

Look me up!

See if you can find the drawings called *Dog*, *Camel* and *Penguin* on the internet. Do you prefer Picasso's drawings or his paintings?

Acting

When I was younger, I loved watching TV comedy shows with my sister on a Sunday morning. And when I first saw a real-life person on the cinema screen, ten feet tall and in such incredible detail . . . well, it was quite a *moment* for me. This love for TV and film got me interested in acting when I was at school, where I studied drama and acted in several school plays and musicals.

Why am I telling you all this?! Well, it's because I want to talk about one very

important part of the art that you see on screen and stage. It's *acting*, the art created by the people who deliver the scripts written by the writers, wear the costumes made by the designers, and interpret the vision of the director – the *actors*.

Actors are *wonderful* creatures, and I have the pleasure of knowing quite a few. It's not an easy job, and although many people think it's very glamorous, it's actually very *tough* and very

UNglamorous – even for Hollywood stars! On film sets, for example, there is often a lot of **waiting around** in between filming scenes, sometimes in the rain and the cold. Actors also work **lonnnnnnng** days, and after a day of shooting will go straight to bed before having to get up early and do it all again.

I have so much **respect** for actors. Shall I tell you a little bit about some people I think are really good at creating this awesome form of art? Maybe you can try and watch some of their work too!

Have you ever seen the TV show **Doctor Who**? If so, maybe you will know of **Ncuti Gatwa**, as he plays the Doctor!

He is an actor who I find to be completely *dazzling* and *captivating*. When he is on screen, I simply can't watch anyone else!

Ncuti was born in **Rwanda**, but moved to **Scotland** with his family when he was just two years old. He studied acting at a really prestigious university and won parts in theatre productions at famous places like *The Globe* in London.

Now, you know how I mentioned acting isn't all glamorous? Well, after he graduated, Ncuti experienced **homelessness**, sleeping on his friend's sofa and borrowing money from another friend to be able to buy food.

But when he was chosen for an important role in a **smash-hit** Netflix series, it completely changed his life.

Ncuti says he hopes that others are inspired by his work in that show, and that he wants to continue to put a spotlight on **diversity** and *inclusion* in Hollywood – which is so very important.

The art of acting is often not just in the actor's *voice*, but in the way they move their *face* and *body* too. Ncuti is so good at acting, he can create a hilarious, snort-inducing scene as well as he can act in a heart-breaking, gut-wrenching moment.

The very best actors, like Ncuti, can change the mood on screen with just a look or a few words.

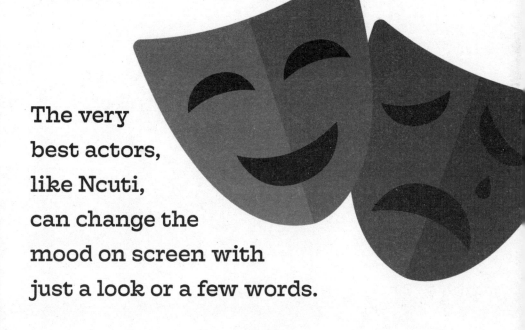

And he isn't just good at changing the *mood* – he's also pretty incredible at changing the type of *character* he is playing.

In his Netflix show, he is acting the part of a high school student, and now, he's playing one of the most iconic TV characters of all time – *Doctor Who*!

You **don't** have to go to university or study acting to create amazing art. Another actor I really admire is *Russell Tovey*, who started acting in children's TV shows at the age of twelve. He created his art by performing in theatre productions when he was still a teenager, too.

I actually saw Russell act in one of his first plays, and I enjoyed his performance so much, I have been following his work ever since.

He is very **natural** as an actor, and what I love the most is how **effortless** he makes the acting seem, both on stage and screen. He doesn't have to be super-dramatic to let you know what his characters are thinking. He does it by way of the **smallest, simplest expressions** on his face. This is much more difficult to do than people might think!

Why not try it for **yourself**? Here's a line to react to, without using words. (You might need that mirror again!)

Using just your *facial expressions*, see if you can convey that you are **angry** AND *sad* at the same time, because your character knows deep down that they are *selfish*, but they're also really *annoyed* at it being pointed out in this way.

> *'Don't you ever think about anyone but yourself?'*

AAAAAAND . . . REACT! Great work there! It's pretty hard to do, right?

So, back to Russell . . . you may have seen him in a few things yourself too. Maybe in *Doctor Who* or *Sherlock*. Or perhaps on *Ru Paul's Drag Race UK* when he was a guest judge.

As well as being a star of acting, Russell also loves **contemporary art**, and collects work from many different artists. He has built an incredible collection – over three hundred pieces!

Of course, it is a complete privilege to be able to own art, but I love the way Russell approaches being a collector, because he is a *fan*, first and foremost.

Russell himself is from a *working-class* background and is a great *champion* for artists. The world of contemporary art can often feel like it is only for rich, upper-class people, but, more and more, we're seeing artists and galleries open their arms (and doors) to people of all backgrounds. It makes the art world a much nicer place because it is more *inclusive* and more *accepting*, and allows artists to find fans from all walks of life.

There's someone else I think is giving the world awesome art with her acting. Her name is *Maisie Williams*.

You may know of her already, but if you don't then I'm sure you will soon, because not only is Maisie a great *actor*, but she is also a great *supporter* of art and people who make it!

She started acting when she was just twelve, in a TV show for adults called *Game of Thrones*. She confesses to having a big imagination and so, when she was acting in the show, she convinced herself that she was actually in the fantasy world created by the show and the books it is based on, and that everything around her was *really* happening.

She is also in a film called ***The New Mutants*** (this one's for young people of fifteen and older, so speak to a grown-up before checking it out) where she plays a character called Rahne Sinclair who can shapeshift into a wolf with superpowers. In a way, she is playing *two* roles in this film, which is *double* the hard work, and also double the imagination to create such different characters!

Away from acting, Maisie was the co-founder of an online platform called *Daisie*, which is designed to help artists and creative people from all types of backgrounds to connect with each other, learn from others, showcase their work and discover projects to collaborate on.

Unlike lots of apps and social media platforms, where users grow their profiles by obtaining high follower counts, Daisie's aim is to bring artists *together* and support them to do amazing work.*

* Daisie is a business too, which means it does cost money to join.

I find it very inspiring to **collaborate** with other people on projects. It's also good to **talk** to people about art you are making or working on — and sometimes to get opinions from people that you trust.

Thanks for **encouraging** artists to work together, Maisie!

ART IN ACTION

Right Joe, I've seen an advert for auditions for the school play . . . what should I do?

Well, you should put your name on the **_audition list_** straight away! Whoever is directing the play will probably give you a piece to learn for the audition, so get learning those lines so you can feel **_confident_** about your performance. Perhaps invite a friend over to practise the lines with you. Remember, being in the cast of a play is like being part of a **team**, so the more you can get used to saying lines in front of people, the better.

It can be a bit **scary** doing an audition – but auditioning is part of being an actor! Plus, don't forget that everyone else auditioning will probably be nervous too. My top tip for overcoming those nerves is to take a **really deep breath** before you launch into your audition piece. Nerves can cause a rush of something called adrenaline to go through our body, which can sometimes make us talk faster. With a few long, deep breaths beforehand, you will naturally speak more **slowly**, which will help in the **delivery** of the lines.

Comedy

I love a **really good laugh**, don't you?

You know – when a mate tells you a really funny joke or story, and you just lose it? I love that feeling . . . that **uncontrollable laughter** which makes your tummy and cheeks hurt.

It's also a great feeling to **make** someone laugh too, isn't it!

Sometimes we do it by accident, but occasionally, when we come up with a **good joke** or **funny face**, it can feel really good to see someone laughing out loud at your antics.

I see **comedy** as a form of art because, much like acting, or music or contemporary art, it creates an *emotional response* from the audience!

Writing comedy is quite different to performing it, but it's art just the same.

Some comedians can do both, and do it alone. Some work with other writers, to help make their jokes even *funnier*.

Either way, there's **huge skill** involved in both of these ways of creating comedic art. There is art in how the comedian **performs** the jokes for their audience, like knowing exactly how long to pause before saying something funny, or how to change their voice or move their body to make their words funnier.

And there is art in **writing** the jokes too. Writing jokes is a bit like writing stories — they need a satisfying beginning, middle and end (which is usually called the **'punchline'**). There's a lot of art that goes into a **laugh**!

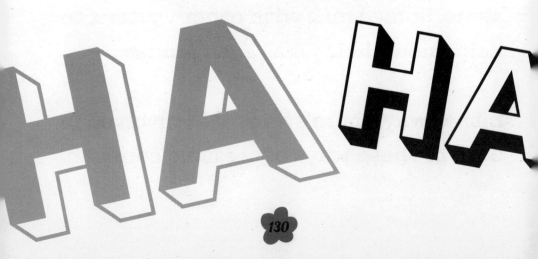

Let me tell you about a few people that never fail to make me laugh, starting with **Rosie Jones**, who is a brilliant comedian and also an author.

HA HA HA

Rosie started her career **behind the scenes** on various TV shows. She would help to write the **scripts** and **jokes**, and would occasionally research the guests who were booked on the programmes and write up notes for the presenters.

After watching comedians on the various shows she was working on, Rosie thought to herself, **I'd like to do that**, and pursued her own career as a stand-up comedian.

Rosie has **ataxic cerebral palsy**, which means she speaks quite slowly.

She incorporates the **rhythm** of her speech into her comedy act, which makes her jokes unique.

After a lot of hard work, Rosie is now a regular guest on many TV comedy shows – including those she used to work on behind the scenes!

In fact, for the *Tokyo Paralympic Games*, Rosie went out to Japan to report on the sport for a comedy show for adults called *The Last Leg*. She did most of her reports in her pyjamas, from her bed, which **instantly** made her reports funny, because when people know they're going to be on TV, they usually dress up and have a fancy-looking background. I love that she made this **performance choice** to create comedy.

Now, you may not have seen Rosie on TV, but you might have read her book! **The Amazing Edie Eckhart** is about eleven-year-old Edie, a girl who has cerebral palsy, like Rosie, and who finds herself accidently cast as the lead in the school play.

As you might guess, Rosie has drawn on a lot of her **own life experiences** for the book, which it makes it very **genuine**, as well as funny.

I love the **energy** and **enthusiasm** that
Rosie brings to her performances,
and how she approaches jokes with a
slightly different point of view, making
us **think a little**, as well as **laugh**.

I also love that she **followed her dream**,
and **achieved it**, too. A truly wonderful
human – and I hope you'll get to read
her words and see her shows in the
future!

Another great comedic artist is *Joe Lycett*. Do you know him? (I don't mean personally . . . although, maybe you do!)

I met Joe many years ago at a fancy dinner. We got to sit next to each other, and after bonding over the fact we were both called Joe (which took up about 6.3 seconds of the dinner) we got to talking about **art** and **comedy** and **writing**.

Joe is another of those naturally funny people that I talked about earlier, someone who can find the comedy in almost anything. His comedy is quite unique – in a slightly off-beat way – which is great, because we all need a little bit of **absurdism** in our lives!

What do I mean by absurdism? Good question! Well, just like there are different kinds of music or dance, there are also **different types** of comedy.

'Observational comedy' pokes fun at everyday life. **'Improv comedy'** is completely made up on the spot, or, 'improvised', often using the audience's suggestions to create jokes. *'Absurdism'* is usually something ridiculous and a bit bizarre. It might be comedy about situations that would just never happen in real life, and yet, because those invented situations are so strange, they are funny.

Joe also uses his comedy to call out companies who have done *wrong* – and to secure *justice* for victims of fraud. This is the basis of his TV show *Joe Lycett's Got Your Back* – in which he mercilessly pranks those who have done wrong. It's funny and entertaining, but he also actually *helps* people, which I think is such a brilliant use of his art.

Another multitalented comedian that I love is **Tim Minchin**.

Have you been lucky enough to see the musical **Matilda**? It's based on the famous book by *Roald Dahl* about a very clever little girl with supernatural powers. Well, if you have, you will have already heard Tim Minchin's comedy because he wrote the *lyrics* for the songs in Matilda! (AND the *music* too. Talk about impressive . . .)

Look me up!

If you *haven't*, you can find some of the songs online.

Tim is an *Australian* comedian, actor, composer and pianist who was born in the UK, but raised in Perth, Australia.

He started out his career **composing music** for documentaries and theatre productions. After several rejections from record labels who said his humorous, clever songs would be too hard to sell to listeners, he decided to create a *show* out of them. The show was a big hit – and suddenly Tim found himself winning **comedy awards** and *touring* the world.

One of the many great
things about Tim is how he
mixes his musical art with his
comedy art, to create a truly
theatrical experience. Plenty
of comedians have mixed
music and comedy before, but
Tim has his own unique style
that he brings to the mix to
make it extra-special.

But, the most impressive thing
about Tim's comedy is his ability
to make *different* audiences laugh.
He can write for grown-ups *and*
for children – and he's great at

both. It's because he takes a pretty similar approach to how he writes and performs his comedy, regardless of the age of the audience.

For example, for *Matilda*, he has written clever, silly, funny songs which rhyme, capturing the thoughts and feelings of **schoolchildren**. And in his adult comedy shows, he tends to sing clever, silly, funny songs, which rhyme, but they're about things which **grown-ups** will find amusing! What a clever guy.

ART IN ACTION

So, how do I set about
trying to make people laugh?

Simple. *Learn some jokes!* You can find
joke books in your local library or in a
bookshop.

Find jokes that make **you** laugh, then
keep practising them until you know
them by heart. Then try them out on
a family member or a friend. See if you

can make them laugh more than once
by telling a few jokes *one after the other*.

And . . . maybe try writing your *own*
jokes! Not all of them will work or be
funny, but writing them and trying
them out is all part of the *fun* and
the *journey* to becoming a comedian.
You can use the joke book as a basis.
Can you work out *why* a particular joke
makes you laugh? You can then use
the *structure* of the joke but make it
personal to you.

For example, if you have a cat, and there was a joke in the book about a cat that goes like this: *What's a cats favourite colour? Purrrrple!* you could change it to be about your own cat.

So, *you* could say . . .

> Hey, Mum, do you know what Mittens' favourite colour is? Purrrrple!

It's a simple trick, but by tweaking the joke to suit your circumstances, it makes it more personal!

Or how about this one? *Why do bees have sticky hair? They use a honeycomb!*

Now what if we just slightly *embellished* this a bit . . .

Hey, buddy, I saw a bee in the garden yesterday and it had sticky hair! I guess it must have been using a honeycomb . . .

By rewriting it like this, I have made it into more of a *story*, and have also made it a little more *personal* too.

Tell your jokes to a few *different people* – your family, friends and maybe some teachers. It's good to see how different people **react**, because remember, like all art, comedy is a very *personal* thing – and different people will find different things funny.

Another tip is to *watch* some comedians and learn from them.

Look at how they stand (or sit). Do they use props? Do they use music? How do they start their shows? Do they pause for a long time before they deliver the punchline to their jokes? How do they end their shows? Does one joke tie in to the joke that comes before? Are they talking about themselves or other people? Are they playing a character?

None of these is the *right or wrong* way, but you might prefer one comedian's style to another.

Dance

When was the last time you *danced*?
Was it in your room? Or maybe at a
party? I bet you didn't realise you were
making art, did you?

The last time I danced was down the
street the other day. It was really early
in the morning and I had some great
music on . . . I felt happy, so I just did a
little shuffle and a quick *bum wiggle*.

Dance can be *majestic*, *beautiful*, *skilful*,
joyful and *magical*. Like the other forms
of art we're talking about in this book,
it can tell wonderful stories and create

an *emotional* response from an audience
– or from you *yourself*, as the dancer.
And there are so many different kinds
of dance, too.

There's ballroom dancing, ballet
dancing, breakdancing, tap dancing,
street dancing, folk dancing . . .

I could go on for pages and pages with
all the different dancing styles there
are in the world! But, the one thing
that is the same about every kind of
dance is that the dancer is using their
body to *tell a story*.

The story has a start, a middle and an end and it might make you feel **different things** at **different times** while you watch it.

I also love how dance and music go hand in hand. (Or maybe that should be foot in foot!) I mean – just think about some of the biggest pop artists around . . . Beyoncé, Dua Lipa, Taylor Swift, Justin Bieber . . . when you see them singing AND dancing, it really does bring their music to life even more.

So, let's talk about **dance as art** – but more specifically, about the **dancers** and **choreographers** (the people who design the sequences of movements for dancers to perform), who make that art.

Firstly, I want to tell you about the choreographer *Matthew Bourne* ...

Oh, sorry – <u>*Sir*</u> *Matthew Bourne* ...
I do apologise!

Matthew trained as a dancer, and danced professionally for fourteen years.

He now runs his own dance companies, creating new shows and **reimagining** classic ballets. His production of a ballet called *Swan Lake* was the **longest running ballet** to be staged in London's West End – and is still considered as one of the best pieces of dance theatre in the world.

But Matthew's version of *Swan Lake* was more than just a beautiful piece of art. It was also **completely unique**, because he used male dancers in the roles that had usually been danced by females.

This had never been done before and caused quite a bit of fuss in the ballet world at the time. The traditional ballet fans didn't like the idea of messing with something that was already considered a masterpiece.

Other ballet lovers argued that Matthew's male *Swan Lake* opened up ballet to a ***new audience***, as well as putting a different perspective on the love story at the heart of the work.

Some of my favourite pieces of Matthew's art are his adaptations of films into dance shows, such as *Edward Scissorhands* and *The Red Shoes*.

I love how these two different art forms – **dance** and *film* – can come together and influence each other.

Elements like the sets and costumes make the show look similar to the original film, but Matthew's choreography uses movement in his dancers' bodies to tell the story, where in the films they would use words.

One of the other things I love most about Matthew is how **supportive** he is of other dancers.

His company, **New Adventures**, delivers workshops for people of all ages and abilities, both as dancers and the next generation of choreographers – which of course, could be YOU!

Look me up!

You can look up **'Matthew Bourne'** on YouTube to find lots of different examples of his choreography.

Think about how the different dances make you *feel*. What *emotions* are being expressed by different moves? Does this *change* when the music changes?

And as a *fun extra activity* – I encourage you to see how many different costumes you can spot ... Matthew's shows always have INCREDIBLE costumes!

Have you ever watched **Strictly Come Dancing** on TV? Yes, me too – lots of times! It's a competition that showcases such a range of different styles of dance – Latin, ballroom, contemporary, street, musical theatre, and more.

One of the stars of the show for me, when she was a *Strictly* dancer, was **Oti Mabuse**.

Oti was born in Pretoria, *South Africa* and actually studied *civil engineering* before training to be a professional ballroom dancer.

This was following in the footsteps of her older sister, Motsi, who is also a professional dancer and a judge on *Strictly*, too!

Oti is so impressive because she is able to go from moving her feet at a hundred miles an hour in the *Charleston*, to gliding smoothly and elegantly across the dancefloor in a *waltz*. She has impeccable timing and rhythm and can create amazing shapes with her body, and of course, on *Strictly*, she had to be the **choreographer** for all the routines she and her partner would dance!

Dances often tell **stories**, and I think Oti is a brilliant storyteller through her art. In her routines, we learn about the characters, their situation and even their emotions.

Look me up!

For example, in her show dance with

Kelvin Fletcher (to 'Shout' by The Isley Brothers, in case you want to look it up) we get a sense that Kelvin's character is a bit *bored* at the beginning, then when the music starts and Oti's character appears, suddenly he's *happy* because he gets to dance!

Oti puts a lot of work into her art, and I really admire that, but I also love the way she always looks like she's enjoying herself while she dances. Isn't that awesome? She is doing something she *loves*, and seems to be enjoying every second of it.

165

Another dancer I really admire is **Steven McRae**. He is a ballet and tap dancer, who also happens to be a *principal dancer* with The Royal Ballet in London.*

* *A principal dancer is a top-ranked dancer in the company, having reached the highest level in both their technical skills and experience.*

I had the pleasure of meeting Steven at *The Royal Opera House* in Covent Garden, London, where *The Royal Ballet* perform.

Steven showed me around the iconic theatre and told me just what it takes to be a professional ballet dancer – HOURS of practice and stretching and practice and stretching. And then some strengthening, **and** a rigorous routine of rehearsals too. I mean HOURS AND HOURS of it!

I was already in awe of all professional dancers, but seeing it up close made me even more impressed by the *dedication* it takes to be able to perform like they do. After all . . .

Steven has performed many great roles on the stage during his career – and I was lucky enough to see him perform in a ballet called *The Nutcracker*. He was so *graceful* while also being so *strong*.

He effortlessly moved across the stage while partnering other dancers, and created the most beautiful shapes and lines with his body.

Some of the *group dances* were breathtaking too, with all the dancers moving in perfect unison, not a single finger or toe out of line.

I was very *moved* watching Steven and the company making their art, and went through many emotions during the ballet.

Look me up!

I wonder how *you* might feel, if you get the chance to watch some of Steven's dancing online?

ART IN ACTION

Right Joe, I've watched *Strictly Come Dancing* and I have practised spinning around my room, how can I make more art through dancing?

For starters, put on your **comfy shoes**, choose some of your *favourite music*, and just bust out your **best moves**!

This could be hip-wiggling, spinning (not toooo fast!) or just shimmying left to right. Maybe even get some friends together and make a **dance party**! Everyone gets to choose a tune or two.

Just remember to drink some **water** if you're dancing a lot – and <u>don't ever</u> try those high kicks or splits you see on *Strictly* without proper training!

If you're keen to learn a **routine**, then there are some great tutorial videos available to watch online.

Look me up!

Why not try *MoveTube* on YouTube?
In one of their videos, you can learn the
dance routine to Justin Timberlake's
'Can't Stop The Feeling' – which is a
brilliant song!

Dance requires a lot of *discipline* and
practice – but if you put the work in,
you will start to see the rewards.

If your school offers dance lessons or
a dance club, why not join up?

Or ask your PE or drama teachers
about dance classes you could join
outside of school.

Poetry

I once thought **poetry** was boring
... written by old people in a weird
ancient language. But, it isn't ANY
of these things! Now, I think of it
as an art form which sits nicely
between writing *stories* and
writing *song lyrics*.

Like all the other types of art
we've looked at together, poetry
has an *immense power* to make
us feel all sorts of emotions. It can
open our minds to a new way of
thinking, or help us understand
how others see the world.

And, if you're still not convinced
that poetry isn't boring, let me
ask you this ...

What do you think of when you think of poetry?

I think of stories told in a rhythm, sometimes in rhyme.

And what do you think of when you think of rap or hip-hop music?

I think of stories told over rhythms, sometimes in rhyme.

Poetry and **rap** are a very similar sort of art, in my opinion! And these two art forms are *definitely* becoming firmer friends.

Still think it's **boring**?!

If a teacher had **told me** when I was at school to look for the **music** in poetry – then I think I would have liked it a lot more.

Now, I **love** exploring the very different art that is created by different poets – whether that's borrowing a poetry collection from the library and reading a new poem whenever I feel like it, or watching videos of poets performing.

Look me up!

Slam poetry battles are really cool!

And so, to some of my *favourite* poets that you might want to check out for yourselves. First up is *Joseph Coelho*, a poet and writer from London.

Joseph wrote his first poem for a competition when he was in Year

Eight. He didn't win, but enjoyed the experience so much he kept writing poems. Thank goodness he did, because now we all get to enjoy them!

Back then, Joseph wrote poems about his feelings; some of them were angry, others were funny. Some were set in other worlds, while others were about everyday life.

One of my favourite poems by Joseph is called '*There Are Things That Lurk In The Library*', in which he encourages us to explore our *own*

stories, as well as those written in books on the shelves. The **rhythm** of the poem is really great. It rises and falls like the dust which is blown off old library books, and it rhymes in places too.

He is also well known for his long poems called *Fairytales Gone Bad*. In these books, he takes a well-known fairytale and gives it a creepy twist, like 'Sleeping Beauty', for example.

In Joe's version, *'Creeping Beauty'*, the main character can see into the future, and one day foresees a world blanketed in vines and a girl covered in thorns. I love this series of poems because they make me laugh and they also help me think in a new way about something I thought I already knew well, like a fairytale.

Joseph often performs his poetry in libraries and schools, especially after he became the *Children's Laureate*!

What's a Children's Laureate, Joe?

Well, it's someone who **writes** or **illustrates** children's books (and sometimes does both!) and who has an **infectious passion** for showing kids how awesome books and reading can be. The Children's Laureate changes every two years, and they will often visit schools and perform readings and answer questions. It's a very special job and very special people are chosen to do it!

Another poet I want to tell you about is **Cecilia Knapp**.

Guess what? Cecilia is a Laureate too! She held the title of *Young People's Laureate for London* between 2020 and 2021, and part of her role was to **raise awareness** of poetry in the capital city – and nationally too.

Cecilia was very keen to hear from people who perhaps hadn't had a chance for their voices to be heard before, or found a way to express themselves. And so, she encouraged young people to try reading and writing poetry, to help others engage with issues that were affecting them. Cecilia says we should write about **whatever we want** to write about, whoever we are, and to do it in our **own** way and style.

As a little side note here – remember how I told you how **Sir Matthew Bourne** was inspired by film and turned this art form into the art form of dance?

Well, poetry can also be inspired by *other* art forms too. Cecilia was inspired to write one of her poems about a piece of sculptural art, a stone carving she saw in a gallery called **Mask**, by artist **Henry Moore**.

Isn't it great that poetry can be about you and your story, but it can ALSO be based on objects that already exist, which have their own story?

Have you ever read anything by *Michael Rosen*? Maybe you were lucky enough to have him visit your school once, because . . . yep . . . he is *ALSO* a Children's Laureate!

I have been reading Michael's books and poetry since I was really young, and still do today. I actually got to meet him a few years ago, when he wrote and recorded a poem for **𝓝ational 𝓟oetry 𝓓ay**, and he was as funny, wise and brilliant as you might expect if you have read his poetry.

What I love the most about Michael's poetic art is the **comedy** and **wonder** he finds in everyday things.

My favourite poem of his – and probably one of his most famous – is **'𝓒hocolate 𝓒ake'**. Have you read it? If you haven't, Michael performs the

poem on YouTube and it's
well worth a watch.

It's the story of how
Michael, as a boy, loved
his mum's chocolate cake
so much that one night he went down
to the kitchen and ate the WHOLE cake
in the middle of the night. He doesn't
tell it in rhyme, but instead there is a
rhythm to the way the words sound
when it is read it out loud, especially in
the way the sounds are **repeated**.

Like many great pieces of art, no matter
how many times I read it or hear the
poem I always get something **new**
from it.

ART IN ACTION

Hey Joe, I've got stuff in my head that I want to write poems about, so how do I get going?

Well, writing poetry can feel a little different, depending on the type of poetry that you want to try and what you want to write about. It's a good idea to experiment a little first.

The first thing to remember about poetry is that it doesn't **have** to rhyme. BUT, it's a fun place to start!

Write down a few words that rhyme. Here's some I've come up with . . .

Mark
Park
Dark
Lark
Lump
Hump
Jump
Bump

Then see if you can make up a few lines of a story using some or all of those words. It can be about anything, and it doesn't even need to make sense! It's all about setting your imagination *freeeeee*! Like this:

> Me and my friend Mark,
> Took our bikes to the park,
> He did a big jump,
> Hit his head, got a lump,
> And was knocked out
> until it turned dark

Another fun thing you could try, if you'd like to have a go at a poem which doesn't rhyme, is writing a *free verse* poem (this is the name for one sort of poem that doesn't rhyme).

Think about what *emotion* you might want to create in your poem. Are there words you could use that would help create that emotion?

Try using just five lines, to tell a little story, using some description and some action. I wanted to create *happiness* in my free verse poem.

I sing in the shower,
and walking down the street,
On the way to work, and in the park.
Oh, the sun is a glowing ball of joy!
The birds are singing their own songs,
From the branches of the old oak tree.

Once you have started writing your own poems, try and pluck up the courage to show some people. Remember, your poems may not be for everyone, but that's OK, because you're writing what YOU want to!

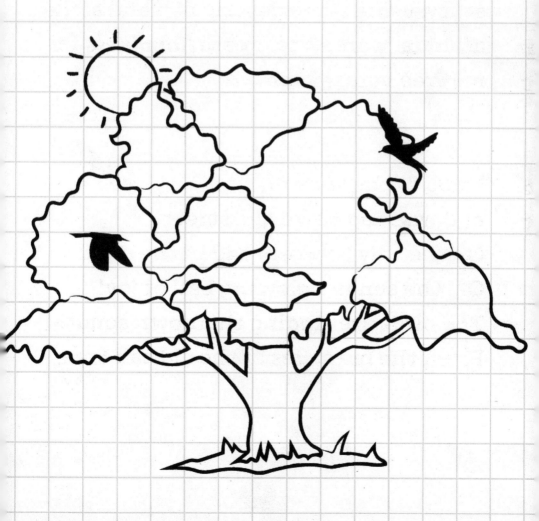

The final word from me . . .

When I sat down to write this book, I wanted to shine a great big spotlight on *art* in lots of *different forms* because I believe it is so important to all of us.

In my opinion, school subjects like *drama*, *art* and *music* are just as important as science, maths and English, and can also bring us lots of useful things.

A subject like *art* for example, can help us to interpret the world around us and to understand a little bit of history too, and studying *music* can actually help our brains and develop reading skills. Research has been done to show that these subjects also help us *explore our emotions* and *expand our imagination!*

I also believe that **The Arts**, as we say when we talk about all different art forms as one big group, are there to be enjoyed by everyone, from all walks of life, whether you are an artist or not.

I hope this book will *inspire you* to look around and discover all the art forms that we come across in our daily lives.

Try it today, maybe? Look around and enjoy the art that you can find in all sorts of different places.

It truly is **everywhere**, we just need to open our eyes and minds to discover it.

And, before this book ends, I just want to talk a little more about you. Yes, YOU! Because you could be someone's favourite artist in the future. (It's possible you already **are** someone's favourite . . . ask your friends!)

Just like how art can be found everywhere around us, art is also about being **creative**, and being creative is something we're doing all the time, whether that's at school, playing a game or even tidying our room!

Remember that we'll have lots of *different ideas* that inspire us to be creative and make art and there is no *right or wrong way* to do it.

So whether you're doodling on a notepad, making up a dance routine to your favourite new song or drumming on some pillows with a couple of spoons, you are letting your creativity run free, and hopefully having a great time doing it.

Being an artist is *not* about becoming rich and famous, it's about doing something you *love*.

BY DOING SOMETHING YOU LOVE, YOU'LL BE HAPPY.

That's the
most important
thing of all.

The Art is Everywhere Artists

As I said earlier, I love it when art is collaborative, and guess what? This book is a collaboration! It has been put together by a whole bunch of fantastic *artists*.

They all do different jobs to make sure the book you've just read looks and reads as brilliantly as it possibly can. Maybe you could be an artist like one of these people when you're older . . .

Illustrator Ellie Hawes created all the amazing illustrations for both inside the book and the cover (which she also designed). I'm sure you'll agree – she's SO talented!

Designer Becky Chilcott helped to guide Ellie in her art and designed the book, making the words and illustrations look fantastic on the inside pages. She also used her artistic skills to choose the fonts that the words are set with. (PS Those FONTS are created by *artists* too!)

Editor Emma Roberts edited my writing to make sure that what I wanted to say was as clear, as fun and as interesting as possible. She used her eagle eye to check that I wasn't repeating myself or saying anything inaccurate, and also checked my spelling (*eek*)!

And *I* wrote the words! I feel very lucky that I have had the chance to make art in this way, about something I am so passionate about. *Isn't art brilliant* . . .

Acknowledgements

It is a dream come true to have this book published, and I want to thank everyone who has bought it, borrowed it, reviewed it and most importantly, read it.

When I was just starting out as a writer, my friend – the brilliant author Adele Parks – gave me so much valuable time and encouragement. I will always be so grateful for your kind words, Adele, which meant so much then, and now. And a big hug to the rest of my 'Costa Crew' – Kit de Waal, Simon Trewin and Sarah Franklin – for your friendship and support.

I feel incredibly lucky and privileged to have worked with such an amazing team of people, without whom this book would not exist.

Firstly, thanks to my publishing team: To Hazel Holmes, for taking a chance on a debut author and on this little book. It is a pleasure to work with you, and to be part of the UCLan family.

207

To my editor, Emma Roberts, for your saint-like patience, wisdom and wonderfulness.

To Becky Chilcott, for your design mastery – and being able to reach into my brain and put exactly what I was thinking on to the page.

To Ellie Hawes, for your incredible illustrations, which have brought my words to life.

To Antonia Wilkinson, Emma Draude and Annabelle Wright – my incredibly hard-working and knowledgeable PR team – and to Graeme Williams and Charlotte Rothwell too!

I want to say a huge thank you to my agent, Gill McLay, who saw something in me and my writing many years ago and has stuck with me ever since. For your guidance, your patience and your encouragement I am forever grateful. Here's to many more years of creative ideas and adventures together!

There are so many friends and colleagues I'd like to thank who have helped me, encouraged me, worked with me and supported me over the years.

Special shout outs to the Big 3, Old Bean, the Cavendish crew, my Brighton and Eastbourne heroes (past and present), the BBC babes and ballers (past and present), the Westminster alumni, all my publishing pals and authors, my magical musician mates, the London lushes and my Spiritlanders.

A special mention for Bill and for Dan, two art lovers who are very much missed.

I wish I could list everyone individually here, but there's just not enough room – you know who you all are though!

Thanks to my amazing parents, David and Yvonne. Your love, guidance and unwavering support mean the world to me, and I will always be grateful to you for helping me discover the joy of books and reading. And to my little sister, Megan (The Pook), the most wonderful caring and brilliant sis a boy could ask for.

To my darling niece, Tabitha, who inspired this book and who I hope will have many creative endeavours throughout her life.

I am so lucky to be surrounded by an amazing, supportive family – all of whom have been so encouraging of this book and my writing. To my grandad 'Joe Senior' (102 and still counting), Toby (BIL), Auntie Pat, Fred, Evelyn, Steph, John and 'the boyz'. To Brenda, Fred, Lauren (SIL), Martin and Dougal, and to my much loved and missed Nana, Grandpa and Grandma, and June and Bob.

Finally, I want to thank my amazing wife Sam. For your boundless love and support, for being my first reader, for always believing in me, for picking me up when I am down, for sharing my love of the arts and for making me the best person I can be. I love you.

About the Author

JOE HADDOW is a drummer, radio producer, writer, podcast host, art collector, music manager and a passionate music fan.

He began rifling through his dad's record collection aged seven, started learning the drums at the age of nine and was acting in Shakespeare plays by age thirteen.

Since then he's been lucky enough to tour the world with his musician pals, and work at the BBC with some of the best people in the radio business.

Joe has judged several literary prizes over the years, appeared on numerous book panels and hosts his own podcast called 'Book Off'. He is a passionate advocate of the arts and has written several articles about different genres of music for children as well as chairing lots events with many brilliant authors.

Joe lives in Brighton with his wife Sam. *Art Is Everywhere* is his first book.

HAVE YOU EVER WONDERED HOW BOOKS ARE MADE?

UCLAN PUBLISHING is an award-winning independent publisher, specialising in Children's and Young Adult books.

Based at The University of Central Lancashire, this Preston-based publisher teaches MA Publishing students how to become industry professionals using the content and resources from its business; students are included at every stage of the publishing process and credited for the work that they contribute.

The business doesn't just help publishing students though. UCLan Publishing has supported the employability and real-life work skills for the University's Illustration, Acting, Translation, Animation, Photography,

Film & TV students and many more. This is the beauty of books and stories; they fuel many other creative industries! The MA Publishing students are able to get involved from day one with the business and  they acquire a behind the scenes experience of what it is like to work for a such a reputable independent.

The MA course was awarded a *Times* Higher Award (2018) for Innovation in the Arts and the business, UCLan Publishing was awarded Best Newcomer at the Independent Publishing Guild (2019) for the ethos of teaching publishing using a commercial publishing house. As the business continues to grow, so too does the student experience upon entering this dynamic Masters course.

 www.uclanpublishing.com
www.uclanpublishing.com/courses/
uclanpublishing@uclan.ac.uk